Excited

Written & Illustrated
by
Nelly Braithwaite

What does Excited Look Like ?

WN

What do you think Excited
looks like ?

What colour is it ?

What shape is it ?

Does it have a sound ?

Does it have a smell?

Which one is Excited ?

What does Excited Feel Like ?

What do you think Excited
feels like ?

What colour is it ?

Is it noisy or quiet ?

Is it big or small ?

Does it taste nice or nasty?

What can make us feel

Excited ?

Can you think of anything that
makes you feel *Excited* ?

What makes you feel

Excited ?

Can you think of when you

have felt Excited ?

Is it good to feel Excited ?

What can feeling

Excited *make us do ?*

Shout Scream and
run around

What can feeling Excited make us do ?

Can you do 3 things that Excited makes us do ?

What sounds might we make ?

What actions might we do ?

Its OK to feel Excited

Everyone feels Excited

sometimes

Your grown ups sometimes

feel Excited

Your Teacher sometimes feel

Excited

Even Monsters feel Excited

sometimes

Run around and
shout !!!

BUT

Only when its safe
and OK

Its ok to run around and shout but only when your grown ups or teachers say you can

If you are at school or home or even in town you cannot run around and scream when your excited

IT CAN BE DANGEROUS

ALWAYS REMEMBER

Its OK to feel Excited

Its how we act that

matters !!

Grown up Notes

Talk with the child about how excitement is ok and how and where to act excited

Discuss wrong and right actions

Discuss what can make them feel excited

Discuss what actions can make others feel excited

Discuss in groups or 1 to 1

Activities to follow on from this book

Find pictures that look exciting

Make up excited song

Think about what holidays are exciting

Talk about what makes you the adult excited

Paint exciting shapes

Its OK to feel book series

Titles include

Angry

Sad

Worried

Excited

Happy

Lonely

&

I don't know how I feel

Its OK to Feel Worried

Its OK to Feel Angry

Printed in Great Britain
by Amazon